Department of Elegy

Department of Elegy

poems

Mary Biddinger

www.blacklawrence.com

Executive Editor: Diane Goettel
Cover & Book Design: Amy Freels

Copyright © 2022 Mary Biddinger
ISBN: 978-1-62557-029-1

Published 2022 by Black Lawrence Press.
Printed in the United States.

For Klaus

CONTENTS

BOOK OF DISCLOSURES

She wanted to taste the fire inside the corn,
cried over photographs of other people's cakes.

Once she punched a cake. Those memories
surface often, like a flood of bus stop pigeons.

She hoped to meet an owl before she died,
did nothing at all to further this agenda item

other than looking up. Curious about clocks,
she asked a lot of questions regarding their guts.

Was there an ocean inside them, for example.
How did the first craftsman know where to lodge

the quiet snore of gears? She asked for holy
water to be distilled down into an adhesive seal

that might ride the forehead all week long
the same way she tumbled her bike into hollows

and ravines regardless of weather. Little reek
of the river which was mostly things left behind.

Once she bit a tree. It was softer than expected.
The blossoms remained unchanged or fell like hail.

THE SLIMNESS OF OUR CHANCES

The delicate status of our couches.
The easily offended elbows of favorite sweaters.

A sudden note that reminds you of fifteen years ago.
Hovering in the first snow outside Hawkeye's.

Lost like a bus in fog. Lost but still dance-ready.
Trying to memorize distinct coordinates.

Giving up in approximately seven minutes.
The unyielding nature of thinking, the hot of glass.

Battle between feeling and reason and feeling.
They call it the upper hand, but it's always down low.

Was there even a DJ, or was the music internal?
Nightmare of an empty hive in a women's restroom.

Nightmare of conversations in a women's restroom.
Don't ask me about my dress or hip bones.

Sometimes it's downright impossible to be authentic.
Every new sentence begins with *Can I talk*?

I was a hair model not a hand or helmet model.
Even my bed was from the Rent-A-Center basement.

Panic about junior high locker combinations.
Will we ever go back into a disconnected payphone.

SUDAFED AND GIN

Listen, I'm falling apart but it was worth it
like eating lunch too fast because you're walking,
or lurching on the deck of a novelty paddle-wheeler
you wanted to exit the moment they pushed off.
These days I'm mostly dry shampoo and concealer
but at least both are effective. Nobody's asking
for my identification but here it is, and the cashier
wears a hoodie with a red polar bear dabbing,
and I've run over both of my feet with the cart yet
in separate collisions. I'm mealy but at least
that's still a meal, it could be worse, grad school
when we'd get wrecked on Sudafed and gin.
Sorry, but I do wish I had more photos from back
then, and not just the PVC jumpsuit or halter
built of metal loops. You won't believe this but
I never thought about the future much. Lost
four or so years down the hole of a blood-mouth
mistaken for a lake. I was dreaming of a man who
ran relatively clean, like a lawnmower engine.

HEAVEN AND ITS ORANGE FLOWERS

Are you my ghost, I asked the water bucket, the Angelus,
a beard of moss grown over a statue's shoulder,

the concept of true friendship, a Rand McNally atlas so
trip-worn it could double as sheets for a doll bed.

The answer was *no*, so I shoved my fist into a hill.
Dropped my tiny beaded purse into the mall's atrium

fountain. Went back to the wing buffet, but it vanished
along with a major thoroughfare and creek

where I once fished illegally for legendary night bass.
I read a novel where butterflies grew plate-sized

and people congregated on rooftops to best view
burning woods from a distance. In the scrap cabin of

my ghost, the curtains roiled with fire, not as cleansing
or like a dancer with a pole-ribbon, but a holy

fire. *Should I take some*, I asked my ghost, who
at this point was purely hypothetical, *Should I go next*,

and then regretted the thought, like when I dropped
a blood-hue marker onto my gingham pants.

It's something impossible to retract. A neighbor
lamented how heaven is so greedy, but she picked all

the orange flowers from our bush. If my ghost
was a piece of debris, I would broom it away but not

forever. I thought my ghost was tangled in a kite.
Braided like a twine-knot baby beside the river's bed.

BITCH WIRE

I was becoming the person with many slips of paper
in her purse. Sobriety adjacent, sandal-wearing,
country fling garden instead of beastly wild pocket.
Maybe in the dream I wore a wire, recorded
my own heart-flex. So many of us want this episode
to end, but it's beyond live, and the coyotes just
pups in an abandoned snowplow tire, dots of polish
on plastic frost. We all compared our levels
of preservation, the goal to resist change like a hill
pounded yearly by weeds. Some mechanism
got me from one point to another, adolescent bus
entering but not exiting the damp underpass
tagged *Stairway to Heaven* back when relevant.
Like many, I poured my best years into
a Springform pan, but they were stupid years.

BOOK OF MILD REGRETS

Here I am, fretting over whether it's okay
to take a second Zyrtec, when fifteen years ago

I downed a pill nicknamed *El Capitan* while
a woman I just met shaved my head with a knife.

It was clear I would never become a Fly Girl
because the decade was off, but my greatest hits

still snapped on like a trustworthy lantern.
Today I apply several coatings of organic spray

proven to further cleanse small batch basil
I vetted at Whole Foods, when almost yesterday

my amateur chainmail had me swallowing
half a marsh in one night, my friend disappeared

past the gorge, a man with sufficient facial
metal to be characterized as a homemade weapon.

Something spiked that was spiked, noise
eating itself beneath flat rocks. And why is it now

I can't settle on a single laundry detergent
but keep replacing what I have with what seems

milder, like the time I cried for sixteen hours
over a photograph of a Chincoteague pony, lodged

between the fence and the hillside, fetlocks
hammered by street mud. When I take my clothes

off and iron them better, when I recycle fifty
sheets of paper for one italic comma, maybe I pay

some forgotten bar tab. Like the time I fell
straight through a mirror imported from Galway.

A BACKPACK FULL OF KNIVES

Even the songbirds that usually lurked our yard
were vacationing in France or posting montages

of crumbles baked from scratch with fresh-fallen
stone fruit. Imagine: a decade ago I'm declared

"a nascent Chekhov" and "a thunderstorm without
the cliché of lightning." Then today, marooned

in a coterie of damp dishrags, unsure which way
to hold a restaurant menu. My former roommate

sends a birthday note all the way from Mykonos:
all emojis. Double entendre, perhaps unintentional.

Also in my inbox: screenshot from notorious Cori.
My apron is wet and this time I don't want it to be.

Email from Brian of the Tennessee encounter, rest
stop where he asked me to guard his caged quail.

I was the Lake Superior of our workshop: forgotten
and cold, always on top. When I passed out photos

to accompany my story, you could smell developer
on my fingers. Not the cocaine or patchouli or Cori

who my classmates believed was a pet mouse, not
a backpack full of knives. My high school English

teacher is now vacationing for six weeks in Slovenia,
despite a salary the size of a mini bag of pistachios,

and she boasts about a simple scallion and rye toast
lunch. I'm still figuring out how to sharpen a blade.

BEAR-PROOF

It was like every reed in the marsh was on fire
with beetles, the ground temporary, clouds a concept

invented by a designer who had been awake all
night drinking schnapps from the cap of the schnapps

bottle. I was afraid to look up my symptoms
next to a bear-proof trash bin, feared I belonged in there.

How long until everyone else got the message
while I was reading the inscription on a bench, another

corporate sponsor disguised as a fallen neighbor.
People thought I was weird still using a radar detector

but they saved two dollars a month downloading
contents of their fingernails into a shared spreadsheet.

The horizon remained true to form but was not
straight. Nothing was. I turned each mosquito over to

inspect for a minuscule battery compartment.
The sun declined a push notification to glide down.

HEAVEN AND ITS TEENAGE RIOT

One woman smelled like honey, the other like Funyuns.
I hadn't started carrying a purse yet, kept a check safe

in my sports bra. When house lights turned off I was not
centered. But nobody waits for a shadow to catch up.

One woman took measurements, the other extracted
feathers from a gallon bag. What exactly was I learning

aside from how to lean? My unremarkable thighs
clanged together like volumes of a fresh encyclopedia.

I wondered how many people had touched the clipboard.
Back then people still actively licked their fingers.

I walked everywhere, considered a coat demeaning.
My street had more boards than windows, a stray rooster.

Thinking about the moon brought collective nausea.
It was 1990 and we spent zero time pondering the future.

People always asked if I had a fever. I tested poorly.
When the flood lights powered on it felt like spit falling.

Basically it was a life with very little context beyond
yes or no. They assigned me a leotard thinner than a mask.

The only taboo was braids so loose they resembled grain.
A phone was a thing with square buttons, a wall mount.

The "hangout" a bald fire pit by warehouse tracks.
Getting high meant becoming happy, and I aspired to it.

TEST OF FORTITUDE

Wherever you've gone I hope you're still hot
and reading novels the way some attack puddings,

the city slightly more aloof but still desperate
because of all the phone light. Maybe an adolescent

like yesteryear-you is gazing at the ice trash
in Lake Erie thinking it's a ladder lying about depth.

I wonder if shoes have become progressively
quieter or if that's just me, situated on the outer edge

of the opposite of a half-pipe, witnessing coupons
expire or spreadsheets corrupt, pining for the plastic

grapes that decorated each table in the old pasta
joint. We pinched them because they bounced back.

I recall tests of fortitude that involved a shaker
of red pepper flakes, Whitney cranked scream-level.

Whatever new occupation you have, besides
the coffin you always aspired to, and wrote heavily

about back when still alert enough to catch
a tennis ball lobbed over a bus by an alcoholic nun

you befriended at the Osco, I hope you're cool
enough to replace your corduroys seasonally, conceal

an empty container of Old Style in the petunias
while conducting official business at 24 Hr Cashland.

Or maybe you've fallen of the screen, flushed
and traded for someone who looked better on paper.

I FOUND YOUR DIARY AND IT WAS BLANK

Things were supposed to get settled
like one nest into another nest,
one account licking the cheek of another
then disappearing for good.
One shoe plummeting into the canal as
its mate remained heel-stuck,
a customer dropping a laminated
menu the moment the last lobster fled
its tank for a sewer, some woman
in her bathtub awaiting a blindfold.
Noise in a perforated sheet of electronic
drumbeat, a figure spinning in fringe,
three people dressed in fake regalia
weeping. Settled like a camera that did
not make people feel sticky,
one branch exacting a scratch like
a crowd of fingernails. How did my
arm taste? Was it like slapping a book
open or dropping treasured photos
into a soup terrine, was it encrypted,
bird-burdened, hastened by concepts
imagined in lab coats? Or settled
like a forgettable character invented
out of spite or misunderstanding,
like some hybrid fruit that looks fresh
only in its ornamental plastic trap.

MINOR CRIMES

We tried a little mild vandalism
like turning the lights off hard,
slamming a sandwich together,
commanding the bus to fuck off
with a slap. It didn't feel right but
maybe nothing felt right, snow
expected but now nearly stacked
to the higher floors of richer
buildings, where a dim old man
awaited the trickle of soup from
a ladle. It's impossible to recall
what my boots looked like or
how many times my forgotten
wool scarf needed to be looped,
or even where I held cash so
that when a gust blasted off
the lake it didn't turn into yet
another sky-vaulting pigeon.
We thought about attempting
some embezzlement but that
sounded so intimate nobody
could consider it controversial.
Once I took a half rack of new
clothes onto the bus and kids
thought I was plain sick, then

I had to walk two blocks while
the hangers played their knife
game. But somehow neither of
my hands hurt from that now.

HEAVEN HAS YOUR FRIENDS, WON'T GIVE THEM BACK

When did the dance floor become proverbial, not literal?

The same year I went right through the art, rather than gazing at it.

A girl was high and tumbled down the metal staircase and died.

Thankfully she wasn't one of mine, but she could have been.

I worked the coat check with such reverence it was a university.

At my desk I felt like double lives were too few to be accurate.

Blended concealer into the zipper-ridges left by a sleeping bag.

Nobody doubted my authenticity, but found me too welcoming.

I harvested a new scowl, learned a more heroic eyeliner swoop.

Volunteered to stand as a stall door when a girl became sick.

Withheld my most riveting dance moves until off the clock.

The DJ flipped on the light in his booth and I lit two cigarettes.

Used to be the greatest tragedies were overdose and car wreck.

Once we sped past a crash before the police arrived (drugs, drugs).

We'd all toss fives into a plastic pitcher, sign a scrapbook page.

But then my friends were gunshots and knives and river bricks.

I wanted to know where they were going when they got lost.

Scraped from the basement of a burned-out apartment building.

Fished out of the gorge against their will and days too late.

PERHAPS THIS IS FOR YOU

The enemy of rice is the sea.
An ocean has no arm since it is
an arm. No longer having to piss
outdoors, I'm tame like a curtain.
People miss the way things hurt.
Just blame it on the barometer,
epidemic of shoplifted bikinis.
Articles calling every bystander
a true hero. Math textbooks nix
the formula for target scents:
Roman candle, radish, wet paw.
I misunderstood what was meant
by *vaudeville*. It was not an act.
But everything turned out okay.

OPEN LETTER ON ABSENT FRIENDS

Some people bid on secondhand mandolins after drinking tequila
or print off a hundred photos of the gang's last raucous outing
to hand out at the current outing, far more sparse and depressing
because everyone quit smoking and eating meat and of course
no more lines blown off CD jewel cases because all the music is
digital and we're either drug tested regularly or sworn straight
edge and barely capable of finishing a twelve-ounce Diet Pepsi.
A few of us inscribe thoughtful notes on the Facebook walls
of absent friends, but others say shit like *We Gotta Hang Soon
Dude* when the dude has been dust for a decade, or tag a lost
comrade in a photo from Florida in 1993, but not nostalgically.
I'm most guilty of using Google Earth to check up on certain
intersections, but not because I am still burned over my wallet
tossed into a creek by someone who shortly thereafter lost
herself across the Michigan-Ohio border. Some of us tried to
pour one out for her, but it was November and blew back,
much like a petty nag on a memorial Instagram post intended
to crystallize the beauty of our collective youth. All of us
washed our clothes in a trashcan and hung them off the porch.
The entire gang heaved into the street on the evening later
called *Laced Tuesday*. We had no photos from the time Ted
stole Carly's ID and cash and I brandished my bike chain.
When your friends have perished under tragic circumstances
eventually they become like beloved characters from books.
You recall being really close in a room, queasy, unsteady or
hot, and then you wake up and your dress is on the floor.

A COMMON QUAIL

I was a hideous church. I did not even
need to try. My empathy and my apathy
squared off opposite blocks of Western
Avenue, or maybe they were two sides
of a really dull coin. I wanted rituals so
I could hate them. Went to movies just
so I could exit the emergency door into
pure bleached afternoon light. What use
was an apron if nothing was simmering
to catastrophe? Boots damp in the toes,
wet ends of hair, renegade noodle arcs
that slam their oils across blank checks.
I was a common quail that wanted to be
cute, but was actually hunted for food.
When I was a child I wanted nothing
else than to close the night like a door.

LIVES OF THE DEAD

Where would we be without you, Savannah, who just had to step out
of a car and some angel-man would appear with automatic transaxle
fluid and a few tools, while your nightwear fluttered around you like
something in a painting not made by amateurs? And of course that's
not your real name, but the intersection is true, and so is the angel-man.
Thanks for sending him to my hospital room where I could make out
a silhouette of the new occupant of my former apartment, across
the emergency road and snowy lawn. When the angel-man pushed
morphine into my arm I vowed to forgive everyone, especially you.
Savannah, I braided your hair while you were asleep and never once
imagined you were a mannequin. From what I understand, nobody
else braided your hair, and within a decade you were small enough
to fit into a cigar box like the one where we hid favorite bracelets,
a hit or two of white blotter. It's hard when a dead friend's name
is also something else, and you have to talk about that city, correct
someone's spelling in an essay and it stings. We once walked six
miles with my awful DOS machine in a wagon, and when the repair
people welcomed us it felt like a completely different planet with
a little less evil, those hippies clustered around obsolete IBM towers,
Led Zeppelin on a tape deck, some questionable Rice Krispie treats.
You wrapped us in their blue hammock's belly, lit incense fronds.
I would like to imagine you're still there right now, waiting for me.

HEAVEN AND ITS CREDENTIALS

For six months or so I coped by fixing everything, like a stranger's
backpack strap on the subway, the clacking issue with the bar toilet,

some guy's plastic abomination that was supposed to be a pirate ship
for kids but looked more like a poorly-conceived explosive melon.

I kept up my research project on the *flâneur*, because if there's one
thing you need after sobbing over obituaries it's the spirit of a dandy

from another century. Certain days librarians at the Newberry pegged
me for just another drug seeker, but I had my impressive credentials.

A dirty-haired girl was crying into a Québécois text and I approached
her with Starlight mints and an attempt at translations. So when you

claim that I misspent five years being awful and calling it my art, it's
neither true nor false. And today I walk into Whole Foods ready to

purchase a snack that's mostly air, with my list primarily of leaves
and clear fluids, and a tidal wave of fan heat and *Jane Says* nails

me to the door. It's my walk-up music, a yoga mom careens her
stroller away from me, and every lemon I lift has stem-end rot.

DISHES OF THE AFTERLIFE

None of the good luck foods suited us, so we pretended luck didn't exist
though clearly it did. Yet who is lucky when fortune is tied to pork?

My friends and I tried to throw a party but the details were tough so we
just watched a few ducks float down the ditch until it got too dark.

Of course we thought the cat got out, and Carly screamed, but then he
materialized in slinky velvet beneath a box that once housed a case

of instant ramen. Of the seven present that night—fashioning aimless
mixed drinks with cherry brandy and Sprite, attempting blackjack

with little understanding of rules—only five made it to thirty. Bored
disemboweling pizza rolls and fighting over a turntable, mad

someone stole a beloved wool sweater or tore the corner of a killer
whale poster, did we have any sense of what an eternity meant?

Dishes of the afterlife differ between cultures but my grandmother
never passed up a chance to slander birds, so no chicken or quail

on the docket as we low-key avoid talking about important things.
I'm wishing I had not burned the photo of Savannah dressed as

a Victorian ghost, which would be an improvement compared to
present, where she occupies some urn or ashtray. We had no

idea of permanence, anything could be disappeared in a flaming
sink, and why she stepped down the stairs while the smoke

stuttered up we'll never know. Of all the horoscopes one might
consult for the new year, none pinches the top of your arm

and maybe that's wrong. My grandmother boiled everything past
recognition. We are still waiting for a burner to finally ignite.

WELL, MAYBE

Let's say you have an extraordinary need
to visit the sea, an insatiable desire to brush

your hand through a chandelier's beard.
Simply thinking about my calendar at home

brought joy, like when someone removes
the lead apron from your body and all rises.

The river had confidence, which I lacked,
but that was no surprise, since it was longer.

In my memory we made it to the shore
but there's no recall of what we read or ate.

Sea birds were like dirty linen napkins
at the edge of a tabletop. All diners absent

because the dishes kept pulling back
into the kitchen, where everything rattled

a beach dirge to lost boats and faces,
eternal physics of a blanket snapped high.

BOOK OF MISDEEDS

You'll find this hard to believe, but we used to pop a little cylinder out of a camera
and hand it over to a stranger who would unfurl it, and then we would pick up
a heap of warm photos, take them home, and paste them onto thick colored paper
with stickers or foil flourishes, and then we would add text with metallic pen,
let it dry, and get this: photograph the page full of photographs and send the photo
to a friend who was in several of the photographs. The friend on the left. She's
not sure if her shirt is cropped or just too short. At the point of capture her tattoos
are not covered up, but in a few years nobody will see them in public. They'll
say (incorrectly) she got married again and (correctly) she's a totally new person
now, the kind who glues all of her misdeeds onto figurative poster board then
carries those displays in tri-fold along on boating trips or to church or fundraisers
where she has to be charming for long periods at a time. They might claim that
her new incarnation bakes, knits, wears light denim jeans with blouses tucked in,
but anyone who has seen that scrapbook page knows all of those items are untrue.
You may want to believe people can change, but sometimes when driving at night
we consider getting off at the wrong exit, and by getting off at the wrong exit
we mean revisiting a long-lost hustle, like a past friend who once looked like two
different people depending on the day and angle, the weather and the decade.

A GENTLE REMINDER

Once I figured out the coat was filled with feathers I couldn't stop
thinking about it. Slid myself into a bright pond to reverse the burn.

Slipped a dental instrument into my pocket for later, ripping just
a peek of a hole, enough to get a sniff of feathers or a cheek-wisp.

I woke strikingly aware of my skeleton and how it was not at rest.
As I slept it pretended to sleep but really left and watched the moon

from our lawn like a restless neighbor. For the New Year, I vowed
I would cease sleeping on my arms. They were mad, and so was I.

Everything kept kicking me over as I crouched. Even the feathers
held a smell that didn't belong to me or to the house: like eye drops

with a hint of melon rind. Typically I was a fine storyteller, yet now
hardly anyone stuck around long enough for a coffin to creak open.

When I plugged my nose I swore I heard the feathers next to bones
but seams were still intact, the zipper gleam a railway to my chin.

BOOK OF THE SEA

Something flew out of me
like a spindle of ribbon, only

it was a series of sounds
and they trapped it in a room

with glass walls and foam
ceiling, and then it belonged

to them. I was truly self-
conscious scrambling the sea

wall, even in my element.
As a toddler they had to angle

me out with a mesh bag
like reclaiming a sharp artifact,

much in the way I begged
a DJ both to play and not to play

what was mostly my song:
once at a wedding of pink carpet

and once after I stepped
into my transom of barbed wire.

That spindle of ribbon
was a stone that looks gemlike

only under water. Waiver
after waiver arrived at what was

years ago my apartment,
then a mailer with cash. They say

some hungry girl tore it
lengthwise, bought a lobster roll

and pollution haze lipstick
with those taped-together twenties.

GHOSTWRITER

The hawk was clearly in distress—I knew this because I was, too.
Somehow traffic seemed to increase or get faster, mostly pickups.
To this day I still worry I haven't locked my car, shut the burner.
Harbored a dream of ghostwriting novels about animals, but not
that hawk and not that day, my hair was dirty and in a catastrophic
up-do. I was wearing a sweater from 1996 and it was not 1996 or
even close. How I envied people who did their lives correctly, not
like a sitcom with a thousand loose threads: fallings-down, trains
dramatically entered and departed, actual guns, furious scrubbing
of upholstered furniture. I'd only had a few memorable junctures
that were clearly critical. I thought of this as I wrapped my hands
in a sack left under a park bench. Conventional education offers
zero insights. Perhaps it would feel cleaner to live up in the trees.

MORE BEAUTIFUL THAN GOD

It was sad—we were all waiting for Carly's relationship to fall apart.
When she posted another photo of roses from her husband we rolled

eyes so hard our skulls vibrated a little. I recalled my academic paper
on how some people might seem like heroes in the past, but are really

incompatible with present life, what with open container laws, tagged
photos on social media, and unwashed hair as meditation practice not

symptom of vagrancy. I presented that paper in my friend's business
suit, which I had to replace after setting a lit Camel Light on the lapel.

In case you were wondering, it was burgundy wool, almost sangria,
which I consumed in ungodly quantities while rehashing highlights

of the Q&A, which was mostly former professors arguing symbols.
Carly says her present relationship is devoid of all argument, lambs

brushing up against each other in the pasture, weekly hot pedicures
and wet yoga, the husband telling her she's more beautiful than god,

and hopefully neither of them has a background in baroque painting
where god resembles a heap of tube socks against a sharp nimbus.

And please don't think for a moment this is schadenfreude, revenge
sparked by our own eventual personages, that we ever pretend we're

in witness protection and the agents assigned us an arbitrary identity
of *dull, fortysomething academic* or *extremely stable urban mother*.

In the latest photomontage Carly and her husband recreate proposal
shoot poses, and I recall holding her jaw open once when wracked

by strychnine. We had to tie her to a chair but she dragged the chair.
The night that skinhead cornered her at the bodega and I had to beg

cops to even slow down. Or the time she kept stomping on her hem.
And maybe I am just a bitter nonbeliever, cynical like that day she

came home with an unidentifiable mouse-type animal, and we told
her to just set it outside, to let the autumn weather take its course.

DEPARTMENT OF ELEGY

The elegies began writing themselves.
Naturally, this made us uncomfortable
as cruising a breakfast bar in pajamas
feels both warranted and inappropriate.
I was invited to speak on public radio
but every word had to be some sort of
farewell, and I wasn't sentimental. No,
this job was not about infrastructure as
much as exoskeleton. Classrooms full
of students groaned as I walked past.
Dogs at animal control shushed howls.
Trees just fell, embracing their fate so
readily that I was tempted to evoke all
the elegies of my predecessors. *What
river is not reinvented every morning*
asked the outgoing minister of elegy.
But that was in a prior administration.

BOOK OF TRANSGRESSIONS

Ouch, my future she said and bleached the windowsill
and bleached the bleach bottle then washed her hands
with scratchy soap. Tore out all blatant sex symbols
from *People*, from the microwave operation manual,
covered any switch that resembled a dick. Let earring
holes close up. Flushed nothing down the toilet, ever.
She couldn't have the cashier ring up new underwear,
tampons, the pre-teens at the drug store shoplifting all
the Tootsie Pops they could fit in their saggy bralettes.
A man in swim trunks played a rhythm guitar poolside.
It was an electrical hazard, immediately reported along
with a frontage violation and nude tip of a drink straw.
The sole vote against restoration of the historical bog:
hers. She refused her own lukewarm promotion, nixed
long foods from the menu: bananas, angel hair, even
those horrid "zoodles" that no human actually craves.
Oh fuck, my aesthetic she whispered into a tissue wad.
Eventually Christmas would arrive with its romances.
Maybe she was just hangry and introspective. A candy
ring for somebody else to suck on while you're busy,
a basket of fries too warm to eat but then unappetizing
when cooled. A couple posed on either side of the flag
pole so all she could imagine was lightning or its sick
reverse. She worried about the grease inside her gloves.

THE CLAW OF GOD

Our second thought was, how do we stop all this blood? The radio cranked
to cover the neighbor's nonstop porn bass, a monochromatic lentil soup

hung in somnambulist funk of the crock pot. Did you hesitate? Did we both?
And weren't you supposed to have once been a lifeguard at a country club

where bikini tops and teeth frequently churned up in the filtration system?
It reminded me of the time we arranged to see a condo on the far west side.

Anything can be a bandage a goth song's lyrics claimed, or maybe blood loss
was putting records in my mind. It was literary, but not an imagined event in

a book where someone could shut the cover, take the elevator downstairs,
and walk into a crowd of people never to return. I wondered if you'd wait

one week before writing about this—whether I lived or died right there—
and if you were imagining how you might howl at the angels of my grave.

As soon as the agent opened the front door we knew the condo was wrong.
I would never slice my hand open on a pint glass again, and I would not die

because like an ancient machinery coming to life under the claw of god
you tore your shirt in half and launched into a masterpiece of tourniquets.

The shirt smelled like some other woman's armpits. I kept asking for rice.
My cat became agitated like a ringing phone. I was a do-it-yourself type

which was why I had researched all the condos by pulling public records.
The taxi to the emergency room was steeped in patchouli that made me

nostalgic for the gentle creeps of Ann Arbor. They were pushing people
out of their neighborhoods to gut the buildings and make them condos.

I didn't have to try to push blood out of my hand—it was in your hair
and frescoed on the back of the taxi driver's seat. You said a poem you

were reciting was by Yeats, but it was really a billboard on the horizon.
Maintenance-free living is not a fiction you said into my free shoulder.

SOMETIMES A GHOST IS JUST A GHOST

People today don't care nearly as much about the Olympics because there's more happening.

Only a small percentage of children creep out of the house to pretend-skate on the driveway.

I have no idea why we placed so much faith in poorly drawn cartoons in odd primary colors.

Lunch boxes were metal or plastic, all the hats had pompons on top like they held brains in.

Nobody spit in the ball pit, and characters in costume rarely pinched the customers back.

I dropped my canned goods in the road and nobody scolded me, said *watch the split peas*.

We did not observe national pencil day, a determination of when donuts were mandatory.

Every pair of jeans looked like it was designed by a machine designed by a vengeful ghost.

HEAVEN AND ITS ATMOSPHERE

I think of this weather as "our weather"
and the shudder of blood down my lip

as our weather, and when bulldozers
rip the faces off houses and pitch birds

into the clouds it's into our atmosphere,
and the bathtub I pretend-drown in is our

mock shallows, like when we projected
a movie onto my thighs, or when you ran

to the store in my jeans for pearl onions,
and that was our bodega where I drew

one twenty dollar bill from the ATM or
dropped a handful of change from our

envelope, and I think of countless bus
commutes with a lake over my shoulder

and my purse wedged between our hips,
how as an early adopter of our madness

I was ready for you to undertake multiple
sketches of my night feet in your notebook

which looked like one of our sandwiches
from back when we worked in separate

kitchens across state lines, where weather
was just another damp apron in the grass.

LETTER TO THE EDITOR

In the shower I recall my most shameful sentences.
Wash my legs with a grapefruit gel labeled *user error*.

Recall a liquid crystal watch that kept me up at night.
A candy called "Chuckles" I didn't know how to chew.

I understood some things should not be taken internally.
Hoped I would never be the kind of dancer who ate tape.

Might pose for another gyros poster if not so inauthentic.
I hail from thunder country, with shrub dogs, ant riots.

Could make acceptable conversation about mechanicals.
However, always feared the machines failing in unison.

I no longer wash my hair with soap sweat and warm beer.
Yet sometimes I may fall into the category of "prepper."

Bought a twin-pack of orange cupcakes with my first tips.
Ate them with my left hand at the bus stop in the rain.

Cringe to recollect odd turns of my lesser lectures on art.
And who was I to even open my mouth unless asked.

MISSION STATEMENT

I wanted everything about myself to be gentler:
my demeanor, my impulses, the stiff indigo jeans

I wore everywhere because I could. The flavor
of dinners that issued from our crock pot daily.

So much for violent rice, cinnamon as hot as you
could stand it. Gentler behind the wheel, more

heron than hawk, like a wet mouse seeking cover
under a trembling leaf, not a tilapia with a knife

in a kiddie pool. I was in championship mode
but wanted to be tipping back in a remedial desk.

I dreamed about riding a horse from the inside,
saddle-free. Thought about washing myself

out of the shampoo, getting spat from a discharge
pipe into the slightly less toxic lake. Wished

somebody would yearn to watch my hands move
so I worked them like a leaking bag of flour

not a costumed settler demonstrating the churn.
I would become gentle as a flooded solarium.

COMFORT GRIP

I was only partially invested
which was a natural state
like the woman who triages
three dates on one night
letting the bullet wound sit
in the corridor next to
the scrape or existential funk
which isn't among dances
taught to us in brief practicum
before they cut the lights
so somebody queued Warrant
because a frequent request
brings the sweet comfort grip
of familiarity, though often
bands like that were nostalgic
to a point we lost our cool
and play-barfing into our hair
was like tapping out, lost
revenue or not, eternal bar tab
humping a thick bill pile
on the coffee table, prettiest
credit card wins, invest in
the future now or drive away
in tomorrow's armpit cab
with today's taped cleavage,
recalling how smeared lights
out the window were marvel
to you as a child, now just
signifying another meter click
like a favorite lipstick sinks
into its socket of abstract fire.

TIME'S DEAD FLOWERS

While you were busy tossing your hamburger wrapper out the car window,
writing on walls with a specialty pen invented for carnival silhouette traces,
or recovering that steel hijack necklace you loaned to all your inamoratas,
I dodged surveillance cameras in a ghoul suit, which looked like my flesh.
In your five most recent profile pictures you're wearing a parka, and maybe
I would too if I hadn't yet come to terms with my own immortality, lashed
to the dashboard like a status masthead, but really just a rosary stolen from
a deceased aunt. And maybe where you are it's always winter, though you
never moved from the town where we met, the one where wealthy people
worshipped apples and frequented a retro soda shop for its irritable waters.
We would listen to Bauhaus on vinyl, and you said I'd never appreciate it,
but here we are, with you peddling novelty ice cream cone erasers online,
and me biting my hand conspicuously in the front window of a bungalow
while my novel shits out of the printer and onto the only floor deserving
to hold it, which is raw wood with a moon-crater finish. So I was a lesson
but the kind that rarely makes it into movies that see a real theater, rather
the films you took me to because they were pretentious, set in landscapes
you thought we should casually acquire, slapping down a platinum card
with a cantaloupe in one hand, a bag of charcoal briquettes in the other.
When you photograph your middle-aged food the filter looks like mildew.
A wife leaning against a mossy beach rock in an algae-wracked maillot.
Kids pitching themselves off bleachers with a series of opaque screams.

GRAY HORSE

I wanted to be out in the field
and then I was overwhelmed by the size

of the field, so I wished to be smaller
like the width of a grasshopper

yet even then I would be too large for some
crevices, like the space between

floorboards where the stealth
spiders tucked their legs when anyone

padded by in socks, and though
the room was so dim I wanted no candle

or lantern after lightning hit the window
in my grandfather's study

which had chestnut cork on all the walls
and we only had one guitar

which I took into the bathroom
so embarrassed at what I was attempting

to play, after *Coal Miner's Daughter* lit
me like a hammock left out

in a hail storm, and I would suddenly now
remember riding a gray horse

across the field as a child in new corduroys
while the birds harvested favorite

invisibles and the horizon slipped
out of its off-shoulder blouse and vanished.

BELL IN A BOX

I was ready like a little claw,
ashamed at how much I used to like
mail. I was a bell in a box, a multi-
purpose tool too difficult to use so
people gave up on me. A chipped
lipstick stalk, bubblegum ice cream
cone toppled onto the tile floor.
I used to be like a solitary fawn in
juvenile pajamas, but now only
a sauce that turned out monstrously
and ended up tossed into alley weeds.
It was like the time I attempted to sew
a dress from some curtains but made
an amateur bear trap on accident.
I was three t-shirts, each one uglier
than the last. My hands smelled like
pastries, but tasted of the insides
of gloves and the backs of ears.

HEAVEN AND ITS DEAD LAKE

You thought that happiness was a meat
I had more than given up. The boundaries
were like phantom buoys that turn out to be
fast food cups in the wake. We pondered
how many bodies were submerged in stages
of sleep or death, but the bats reminded us
that it's either the grimy bathtub of your
apartment or the grimy bathtub of afterlife
and only one has scented soap. My body
felt like a tiresome awning, constructed in
some past decade where priorities differed.
Women wore pantyhose and dialed phones
with the eraser end of a pencil. My building
had baroque flourishes that conflicted with
most modern sensibilities, including fresh.
I would sip a glass of lake water gazing out
the window at the lake. My free agency felt
like an invisible rush left behind by a wave.

A RADICAL NOTION

Graffiti on the bridge read: *You have no future in administration.*
My heart opened like a scantron sheet with every bubble filled in.
Society had run out of things to weaponize—even the ugly plums.
I told myself not to think, but it was like spitting into a high creek.
My worries like hot missalettes they shoved into our church arms.
I preferred to take my arms into the woods for a thorough scaring.
Knew it was wrong, but still wanted to eat a cactus heart someday.
Savannah took a cactus out of her blouse and then she disappeared.
Nobody wanted to purchase our grass bracelets, not even out of pity.
The administration retracted the definition of *renewable energy*.

HEAVEN AND ITS CHOPPY WATER

I felt better on a lake as if
otherwise something was missing
like the time we baked with oil
instead of water or tried to trim
the lawn with kitchen scissors.
We owned two lamps and had to
carry them from room to room
like torches. We smelled of Borax
or spider webs, our house mostly
attic space with curtains for doors,
and we'd play a game with friends:
who could sprawl across the bed
then touch all four walls at once.
One time a squirrel sat on the stove
and we just watched. One day rain
coasted under the locked door.
I was either waiting to arrive or
to leave. All night two red beads
on a string slapped their wasp
concert against the screen.

BOOK OF HARD PASSES

I was trying to make my way through another memoir of privilege
as if the author wouldn't eventually have a Wikipedia page stating
her neighborhood and how her parents, before their divorce, spat
dollars into the channel and let her burn royalty checks for kicks.
Once, it's rumored, she met the queen. And as her readers we now
should feel a sense of kinship via headaches, hers caused by jewel
necklaces which pushed on the spine, ours the result of dancing in
a cage for a decade and not knowing better than to whip our hair
for better tips, which we sometimes peeled off the keg-wet floor.
And yeah, we both valued our art and felt like shit when people
in workshop dismissed our experiences as trite or hallucinatory
to the point of tossing the reader out of the narrative by the belt
loops. Apparently the memoirist had some unfortunate meals, or
watched her sweater drift down a river too high to fetch it, but
these are fair experiences for anyone undergoing an adolescence.
And isn't most literature vengeance in some way? For example,
everything I write is for one solitary person and I must attempt
to make the proverbial paper airplane land in that one dusty lap.
Good luck, the people who humiliated the memoirist said, only
it wasn't meant as good luck. We can only hope to become trade
paperbacks someday while the people who accused us of *prose
with line breaks* rather than *truly liminal and enlightened verse*
are still pissing against the same alley wall as in graduate school
hoping for different results. And when they remark online that
my life, or the life of the memoirist, ended up surprisingly banal,

and would we like to submit to an experimental online journal
or perhaps judge a contest gratis, now we're the ones jerking
the trash can away while they are mid-heave, and we drop red
pens onto their latest efforts, hoping, at last, for a little slash.

SNAGGED IN FISHNET

It was time to go home, and then it wasn't.
Every sweater failed at its primary goal
which was simply to cling. We purchased
a quart of hair-colored paint, which later
we peeled from my shoulder like sunburn.
The night was a finger snagged in fishnet.
You had three quarters of a game plan left.
The bus felt too hot but it rocked, bucked.
Flood lights in wet tubs like an emergency.
What did it mean to be *embedded*? Today
I realize it was both a question and answer.
Air and leaves freaked the only statue left
in the park, and I wished I could risk a hit.
Things completed themselves back then.
Weather emptied its pockets into the street.
It never happens now. We're living in one
dirty green winter jacket, and then another.

BARELY THERE

You might be a decent sandwich artist
working with terrible bread, a seamstress

laboring under the light of one candle
constantly igniting the polyester trousers

of your ambition. Every dancer claims
to be classically trained. All intellectuals

aspire to go public. Maybe today you
sell used Hondas, but in the new year it's

refurbished tennis bracelets or feather
tails for remedial ballerinas. Sometimes

a figure skater has to decide between
soup in a novelty bread bowl, or second

place. We all hope to master a spin,
but what do we miss in the meantime

like creating a scene at the laundromat,
shoplifting, engaging in high-stakes tricks?

Any letter that begins "You will not
remember me" should be returned unread.

You might be a talented dancer but
dancing in an awful place, like a baptism

birthday party combo with zero gifts.
Perhaps you've overstated your attributes

in a cover letter, italics and blistering
verbiage, a color photo from better years.

HEAVEN AND ITS STATIC

When I drink amaretto sours I get my old self back
and it's pretty awful. There's a reason we left her
at the bottom of the mountain with a faux soldier.
She's probably still preaching various weak beliefs.
Or wearing that sweater with the metal brackets.
It's amazing we traversed the entire valley on foot
but we were younger and didn't think about feet.
When the wrought iron café chair left waffles all
up and down my ass, I laughed it off, got hungry.
While she was feeling her way out of catacombs
I auditioned a few prospective masseuses. Shame
we had to separate on account of passport drama.
My new incarnation fixed problems preemptively.
Threw out the Dutch baby before its edges burned.
Remained on a couch when the DJ played ABBA.
But then, inevitably, there's a mirrored bathroom
corridor and a stall with a stranger on the phone,
only the call is for me. She puts it on speaker so
even my frenemies can hear the intimate static.
Soap flows directly from dispenser to tile floor.

PERSONAL STATEMENT

After so much time working in a bandage factory
you become a bandage yourself, much like the woods

on their creep closer to abandoned row houses
that sink like grommets into the leather of the block.

Any one person alone is wholly uninteresting, but
fan that punitive gray wool skirt out against a river

and it will be chainmail to the elements. Perhaps you
lose things like your pens, or feeling in fingertips,

but are in no way a loser or lost unless you want to be.
If your days are spent testing the gauze, you might

hope to go home and find a loose beam or triggered
dove in the eaves. Occasionally your own body

is the factory, and the bandages are what you speak
into a series of plastic buckets or letterhead envelopes

which are kept in a locked cabinet much like your own
chest, flecked with disregarded memos or old tape.

TERMS OF AGREEMENT

The man who described himself as a contemporary American novelist
in his biography for the *Nextdoor* neighbors forum hasn't mowed a blade

of his lawn since May, but who cares about that when there are cost-
effective generics to assess, easements to criticize, balking about frontage

which makes nobody else recall nights in the Winchester Mall overflow
lot, the one never used because there were never crowds. Oh, the fronting

executed there. I briefly showed a class a snapshot of some jeans noted
in a poem (I once owned a pair) and my evaluations shuddered. However

we soon moved on to discussing fates of wild horses, which banished
all memories of distressed denim. The woman who typed "HI" in response

to the heated discussion of chipmunk proliferation, or the headstrong
babysitter who uploaded a pic of herself eating two ice cream cones at once:

instantly forgotten. None of them knew I was surrounded by couch
cushions, regarding a sepia portrait of a cherished ex like it was newfound

currency. Back then I had a vague notion that fifteen years later we
would be separated by amateur divorces and lactose intolerance and miles.

Warmed by the heat of our respective pit bulls, we would hang on to
imaginary lockets while reading (again) *Cold Mountain*, like it was secretly

the story of us. But the real story was why the intersection of Rhoades
and Maple was flooding. Perhaps the new mini strip mall, or illegal dumping,

which is how you described it when I dropped my big salad and ghosted
contrary to the terms of our agreement, which were written in gross cursive.

Sometimes I yearn to fill out the rest of my bio, but right now it's mostly
symbols: a wave, a skull, a shark, a daisy that might look nice behind an ear.

BOOST POST

One of the fact checkers insisted on grabbing a handful of my skirt.
It was plaid, or black polyester, it was part of my work uniform or
nurse costume, it was supposed to be a blanket but you use what
you have. The fact checker pressed a red check mark between my
eyes when I said I could make a tent from napkins (I put it on his
lap, I put it over his mouth, his nose, bent his fingers too far back
which made it a little declaration of war, which is still declaration
of war). One of the fact checkers tried an emotional appeal, which
felt unethical under the circumstances, like when a boss calls you
sweetheart but your name is *meanheart*. Famous for locker room
fights, unafraid to tear earrings from lobes, that kind of colleague.
Overalls offer ideal provisions for carrying facts but who even has
a pair anymore? We buried mine with a dead wren up in the front
because lord help all of us if in the next life we have zero wings
to get us out. The fact checker wanted out, but I wanted more out.

AN UNEXCEPTIONAL FACE

Maybe you just need a good thrashing
at the hand of some obscure god

who makes you feel the way food coloring
in a box lit you up in the baking aisle

of childhood, or when you closed eyes in
the gallbladder of car wash spinners

believing you'd been in their midst before.
You spend a lot of time looking into

the sky as if it's an unexceptional face
passed over by a talent agency, cold pond

of gasoline-rainbow waters, a gesture
with no meaning in this particular country

but banned abroad. Maybe we're just
too dirty to worship, or to be worshiped.

HEAVEN AND DIRT

There you go with the crushed velvet and makeshift bracelets,
the judgments and cribbed recipes from major restaurant chains,
assorted creepers wearing your likeness on sweatshirts, checking
your favorite books out of the library just to sniff the pages you
previously sniffed, and your hair that's like a bank of parking
lot snow shoveled from some other more important surface, or
a cape purchased on impulse but it smelled like formaldehyde
so you used it as a sex in the woods blanket instead of sleeping,
the lightning-quick email replies that annoyed even superiors
who were many, considering your station, which had upward
mobility yet you stood behind the curtain instead of in front,
opened the lid of the piano bench instead of revealing the keys,
chewed mango as if you grew up in a mango-less bog, crotch
of the worst maple in all your self-portraits, which were many,
and I recall someone once saying it's hotter to be a bit messed,
for example some history on the skin or lipstick that's trash,
but maybe that was the man who kept fingering my shoulder
blades like they led to some cavern when in fact I was full of
stones and dead owls and recollections that felt like chipped
plaster in the bottom of a padded bra, leaving little mustache
room or input about which boots looked nattier on him, so I
suggested maybe you could roll in with a Cindy Crawford
past prime aesthetic, ordering the bangers and mash without
even perusing the menu, your gilded artichoke pattern tights
and not even a pretense of vegetarianism, the tiny handcuff
earrings you probably slept in, the heap of vines you'd piss
behind while some paying customers observed, shoulders
greased with oil and the shush of dollars dropped into a jar.

ODD MYSTERIES

The newspaper headlines were all about a miraculous rowboat.

Meanwhile I was teaching kids what to do in case of bullets.

Recalled learning about the best furniture to flatten myself under.

But that rowboat had either a mind of its own or some saint.

When we were a canal town bullets were rare, but not rowboats.

Imagine the size of the hats, the blistering spangles and flags.

A local historian bemoaned difficulty of so much entertainment.

I told the kids not to worry about looking stupid on the ground.

First time for me was a bank robbery and all remained so still.

Of course, I'm an import, a compact car with odd mysteries.

Maybe the miraculous rowboat was another flimsy metaphor.

I was surprised at how quietly the alarm rang: a singing bowl.

Then that time at Convenient Mart, or at Western Avenue Park.

My overalls fronted in dust, birds making more birds above.

They say that we all have our moment and should stay ready.

At college everyone was like, *You don't have to clutch your bag.*

Was like, *Take a nap in the grass, hang your coat in the library.*

The miraculous rowboat just a pile of lumber back then, waiting.

But a girl was being shot at that moment behind a corner grocery.

The rowboat was a cherry hoping to get pitted by lightning.

One night it would captain itself across a vast industrial lagoon.

A man on the bus flashed a piece in his sweatpants waistband.

The boat took on water overnight, rocked like no accident.

Ghosts of yesteryear's revelers packed it with yellow lilacs.

RETURNING TO DIRT

I was feeling really good. I had a friend in town. My hair was soft with grief. Hourly the clock tower made me cry but it was an excellent cry, like drinking from a spring. It was cool enough to wear a scarf which is ideal for absorbing tears unless it's real silk. The thought of all those silk worms, oblivious to their ultimate role, was a reason to weep. I was not thinking about the rabbit we saw returning to dirt beneath a mulberry bush. Sometimes I seemed like a character created by a man. Just because you can do something doesn't mean you should. Such as listening to rain on loop. Eventually it will have an effect. My roommate nearly died from standing in rain, and then actually died. I had to throw away every plate in the apartment but didn't have the heart. Instead, a note and a stack. Everything was incomplete. A few grains of salt but not a block.

ANTIQUE FILAMENT

This is the year that I stop answering. Grab the wrong knife
and follow through with it. Tear the doorknob

off the door. I walked into my deepest fear which loomed
like a gown on a hook. Held several prescribed

words at the ready: something about a holiday, quick joke
on swan taxidermy, a pair of Victorian facts.

This is the year I tell everyone how I like wet hinges, trick
bathroom locks you can leave unlocked

if you want company. I said I was waiting for you to come.
The lighting was unrealistically flattering.

Have you ever watched a real clock grind its time, I asked,
not waiting for a reply, recalling a stunned

finch in its stoned spiral out of the rotting crabapple tree.
Maybe we returned to the party like vendors

hovering around a quota. The year already afire, a bucket
of receipts for items that no longer existed

because we banished them. And then a watery anecdote
about paintings atop other paintings, rude

if the artist is within earshot, objectionable when ripped
stockings are still visible beneath a revised

landscape. Somebody put us here and then covered us,
watched as we unbuttoned and stepped out.

GOD'S PLAN

Occasionally I pine for a mild disaster
such as a really loud cough of thunder
followed by wind that tears the scarves
off the lawn, throws patio chairs around
and maybe a contaminated lake barfs up
some sensitive documents or a dead hog.
It's hard not to scream in church, library
map rooms aren't much better, or the ice
rink where music remains in 1982, nacho
machine on the brink of a calamitous fire
but somehow still producing its cheeses
which I will never be able to eat, thanks
to my ancestors who survived on boiled
stones and shags of grasses and sheep's
dreams. Real excitement is a hidden bee
in a box of raspberries, putting the car in
a wrong gear, then gunning it. As a child
I had a placemat emblazoned with photos
of nine different types of scat. Sometimes
I recall it as I recline in the dentist's chair,
pinned down by the lead vestments of joy.

ACKNOWLEDGMENTS

Many thanks to the journals where the following poems first appeared, sometimes in a slightly different form or with a different title:

The Adroit Journal: "A Gentle Reminder" and "I Found Your Diary and It Was Blank"

Allium, A Journal of Poetry & Prose: "Heaven and its Dead Lake" and "Heaven and its Teenage Riot"

Bennington Review: "Antique Filament" and "Heaven and its Orange Flowers"

Black Fork Review: "Personal Statement," "Heaven and its Atmosphere," and "Bell in a Box"

Court Green: "The Slimness of Our Chances"

Crazyhorse: "Department of Elegy" and "Mission Statement"

The Hunger: "Bitch Wire" and "Ghostwriter"

Inter/rupture: "A Common Quail"

The Laurel Review: "Gray Horse," "Heaven and Its Choppy Water," "A Radical Notion," and "Sometimes a Ghost is Just a Ghost"

Poetry: "Book of Disclosures"

Poetry is Currency: "Minor Crimes," "An Unexceptional Face," and "Heaven and Its Static"

Psaltery & Lyre: "God's Plan" and "Odd Mysteries"

Rogue Agent: "Sudafed and Gin"

Shock of the Femme: "Comfort Grip," "Heaven and its Credentials," and "Well, Maybe"

Southern Indiana Review: "Book of Mild Regrets" and "Open Letter on Absent Friends"

Sugar House Review: "Boost Post" and "Terms of Agreement"

Thrush: "Perhaps This Is For You"

Tupelo Quarterly: "Heaven and Dirt"

Waxwing: "Returning to Dirt"

Grateful acknowledgment is made to the Ohio Arts Council for their support through an Individual Excellence Award in 2018, and to the Cleveland Arts Prize for a mid-career award in literature in 2019.

Much gratitude to friends and colleagues for their support: Erica Bernheim, Heather Braun, David Giffels, Mary Grimm, Noor Hindi, Jennifer L. Knox, Robert Krut, Thea Ledendecker, Erika Meitner, Jon Miller, Caryl Pagel, Tricia Springstubb, Gina Ventre, and Marie Vibbert. Special thanks to Susan Grimm and Amy Bracken Sparks.

Rivers, swaying grasses, dark sidewalks, and eternal thanks to my book trailer team, Claire Headland and Gabriella Thompson.

Thank you to Black Lawrence Press, especially Diane Goettel and Angela Leroux-Lindsey, and to designer extraordinaire Amy Freels.

Bountiful appreciation to Julie Brooks Barbour, my fellow noise poet, my first and best reader.

Love and thanks to Eric, Gabi, and Ray.

Mary Biddinger is the author of six previous full-length poetry collections, including *Partial Genius: Prose Poems*. She teaches literature and creative writing at the University of Akron, and serves as poetry and poetics editor for the University of Akron Press. Poems and flash fiction have recently appeared in *Bennington Review*, *Crazyhorse*, *DIAGRAM*, *Gone Lawn*, *Rogue Agent*, *Thrush Poetry Journal*, and *West Trestle Review*, among others. Biddinger has been the recipient of Individual Excellence Awards from the Ohio Arts Council, a National Endowment for the Arts fellowship, and the 2019 Mid-Career Cleveland Arts Prize in literature. Her current project is a flash fiction novella about the adventures of two graduate school roommates in late 1990s Chicago.